LET'S VISIT THE U.S.A.

Let's visit the
U.S.A.

NOEL BARBER

BURKE

ACKNOWLEDGEMENTS

The Publishers and Author would like to thank the following individuals and organisations for permission to reproduce copyright illustrations in this book:

J. Allan Cash; Colour Library International; Keystone Press Agency; Photo-media; Paul Popper Ltd.; Skyport Fotos; the U.S. Information Service and the U.S. Travel Service.

The colour photograph of the Statue of Liberty which appears on the cover is reproduced by kind permission of Fox Photos Ltd.

The Author would also like to record his grateful thanks to Donald Dinsley for his invaluable help in research.

ISBN   0   222   66844   ×   Library Ed.
ISBN   0   222   66856   3   Hardbound cloth Ed.

Burke Publishing Company Limited,
14 John Street, London, W.C.1.
Burke Publishing (Canada) Limited,
73 Six Point Road, Toronto 18, Ontario.
Made and printed by offset in Great Britain by
William Clowes & Sons, Limited, London, Beccles and Colchester.

Contents

Map	6 and 7
Who Are the Americans?	9
The Birth of a Nation	16
Geography and Climate	21
Washington, the Capital City	27
New York, the Tallest City in the World	32
Rivers	37
Railways and Roads	41
Mountains and Deserts	44
The Deep South	49
Crop-growing and Cattle-farming	55
The Vanishing Indians	61
Taming the Wild West	66
Industry and Engineering	70
The Negroes	76
Reaching for the Sky	79
The Two New States	82
Games and Sports	89
The Young Americans	92
Index	94

THE UNITE

CANADA

Alaska inset:
Nome
ALASKA
CANADA
Juneau
0   300

Main map:
CANADA
WASHINGTON
Columbia R.
OREGON
IDAHO
MONTANA
WYOMING
CALIFORNIA
NEVADA
Salt Lake City
UTAH
COLORADO
Colorado R.
PACIFIC
San Francisco
OCEAN
Los Angeles
ARIZONA
NEW
MEXICO
Rio Grande R.
T

Hawaii inset:
MOLOKAI
Honolulu
MAUI
LANAI
HAWAII
0   100

MEXICO

This book is for
Adrienne Jane Dinsley

Who Are the Americans?

The American people are particularly proud of a strange fact about themselves: that one third of the population of 182 million men, women and children who live in this vast, exciting country are, in fact, foreigners.

Certainly, few foreign visitors to the United States feel totally strange amongst the millions of Germans, Italians, British, Poles, Canadians, Scandinavians, Irish and—in smaller numbers—Russians, Czechs, Austrians and Hungarians who make up the American people.

Americans will tell you—with genuine pride—that the American citizen is the product of the "melting-pot" of all Europe. Some Europeans went to the U.S. to escape political or religious persecution; many to better themselves; others out of a spirit of adventure and a belief in the democratic principles of the United States. Later, the Europeans were joined by Chinese and Japanese.

Naturally, the new "Americans" wrote home, telling their friends about the great opportunities awaiting anyone who had the spirit of adventure. And, equally naturally, the men and women who followed tended to settle in parts of the country where they had friends and relations; nowadays, you can often visit a city or a district in America and believe, for a moment, that you are back in Europe.

In Boston, they speak with an English accent; in New Orleans, many of the shop names are in French; stop in any

The American population is made up of people of almost every race and nationality. This section of New York is known as "Chinatown" because so many Chinese live there

street of New York and you are likely to hear workmen arguing in Italian. One district of San Francisco is called "Russian Hill", and the city also has one of the biggest Chinatowns outside China. Further south, around Los Angeles, the Mexican and Spanish-style design of many houses shows the influence of South America. In the great rolling acres of the Mid-West —which is fine farming country—you will find yourself among Scandinavians, Germans and Dutch.

These, then, are the Americans—often they are men and women born outside the country they now call their own. They are loyal and patriotic, but the ties with the homeland— even the homeland of three generations ago—have not been

10

completely severed. The new Americans are proud of being American, but they will boast of their ancestry.

Come to New York on St Patrick's Day: you might think that on March 17 only the Irish lived there. Traffic is halted as fife bands lead crowds of men and women, wearing shamrocks, swinging down Fifth Avenue. Indeed, it was only recently that New York stopped the Irish changing the painted white lines down the city streets to green on St Patrick's Day.

But see the same city—and many of the other large cities—in January, and you will find nearly one million Russians celebrating their own Christmas, while at the same time the Chinese are celebrating their New Year.

On St George's Day it is Britain's turn; many towns hold

A St Patrick's day parade in New York

Two of the "true Americans". The little boy is dressed more like a cowboy than an Indian; his mother is wearing traditional costume

special church services in which a message from the Queen is read by the British consul.

The Italians—there are two million in New York alone—are always parading on feast and saints' days throughout America. In fact, almost any day in the year sees some group of "Americans" celebrating an event linked with their old country.

But who are the true Americans? It is not an easy question to answer, for officially the U.S. Government recognises any citizen of the United States as an American, but classifies some citizens as "foreign" if they were either born outside the United States or are the children of foreign-born parents.

To be strictly accurate, of course, there are really only 400,000 true Americans. They are all who are left of the Red Indian tribes Columbus met when he landed in America. For this handful of men and women are the only direct descendants of the original inhabitants. It is interesting to note that they are misnamed—they are certainly not Indians. Columbus and his white explorers were mystified by the strange copper-coloured, high-cheekboned and scantily clad men whom they met. They did not know what land they had discovered and decided they must have reached the Indies, and that the natives were Indians.

It is one of the tragedies of the American continent that so few of the native inhabitants are left in existence. At first, the Indians were friendly to the white men and welcomed them. But greed, cruelty and treachery on the part of the discoverers soon led to hatred and war—and to the extermination of many Indian tribes.

There is another important ingredient in the strange mixture that makes up the American people. Nearly 18 million inhabitants are Negroes—descendants of the slaves imported from Africa during the days when America was a British colony.

If you had been visiting the United States before the First World War (1914–1918), you would have seen large numbers of Negroes only in the South, working on the tobacco and cotton plantations where slaves provided the necessary labour in a country that was still under-populated and under-developed.

In those days, the few Negroes in the North were mainly bought and sold as personal servants; the rest stayed in the South as slaves until, in 1863, Abraham Lincoln gave them their freedom.

Though freed, few at first moved away from the South, until the booming war factories of the First World War tempted them to the industrial North with its promise of better pay. The expanding era of the 1920s with fast-growing industries, producing items such as the motor-car which was then beginning to be mass-produced, turned the trickle of Negroes leaving the South into a flood.

Today, the Negro population is scattered across the country. Indeed, the last census showed that Chicago, for example, has a Negro population approaching one million, while there are over one and a half million Negroes in New York.

The "melting-pot" of different races has made the Americans the friendliest people on earth, and it is easy to understand why. You can imagine lonely and apprehensive new settlers landing in those early days on the shores of a strange country, probably not even speaking "American". How much it must have meant to them to find a friend to give them a helping hand!

Because of the dangers, and of the way people had to rough it in the new country, friendship became, in a strange sort of way, a code of honour; for who could know if the man opposite might not be badly in need of help.

Times have changed; but the habits have persisted, so that today—if you are a visitor to America—total strangers will often greet you, tell you their first names, and ask if they can be of service.

All these children are American, whether black, white or brown

The Birth of a Nation

Just what is the United States of America—and how did it come into existence? It is a vast country, covering half a continent—a country which was supposed to have been discovered by Christopher Columbus in October, 1492, although there is strong evidence that the land was actually discovered in 1003 by the Viking Leif Ericson, a great sailor who set off west from Greenland to seek a new land. He and his crew first sighted Newfoundland, and from there they sailed along the coast to the mainland of North America. Ericson named the country Vinland.

Neither Ericson nor Columbus realised just what they had discovered. Neither made any profit from their discovery, for it was not until 1607 that the first real settlement was established on the east coast of Virginia, a new colony which was named after Queen Elizabeth I, the Virgin Queen. It was founded by a private British firm, the London Company.

The London Company pioneers were followed by the Pilgrim Fathers whose ship, the *Mayflower*, landed at what is now Massachusetts in December, 1620, after a three-month voyage from Britain. Massachusetts became the second colony. Settlements in eleven other areas had been started by 1700.

Yet, even by that time, none of the settlers had any idea of the vastness of the country they were colonising.

Many of the settlers were the victims of persecution—men such as William Penn, who played a leading part in the founding of Pennsylvania. Penn went to America in 1676 after having been several times committed to prison by the English courts; on one occasion for publishing certain books setting forth his religious beliefs, which, as he was a Quaker, went against those of the established Church; on another occasion, for refusing to remove his hat in Court before his "superiors".

But how was the United States formed from that tiny colony of Virginia, and the other twelve settlements that followed?

There had been bitter trouble between the settlers and King George III in England. The colonists felt they were being treated unjustly, that they were being too heavily taxed. In addition, they felt themselves bounded by countless petty restrictions; so they became more and more rebellious. Matters came to a head in an incident known as The Boston Tea Party.

Boston was thought of by the people as the birthplace of their liberty—and had been since 1630 when John Winthrop and a band of eight hundred Puritans from England landed there to seek a new life away from religious and political turmoil. They established a new town, and named it after Boston in Lincolnshire, England.

It was here, on December 16, 1773, a freezing, wet day, that seven thousand Bostonians protested against the unloading of three British vessels carrying East India tea. They were really protesting about the Tea Act which had been passed earlier that year, through which Britain had given the East India Company a monopoly on tea-trading to the colonies.

The Americans felt it was their right to buy their tea where they wanted. They demanded that the ships be sent back to England with their cargoes. When the demand was refused, men and boys disguised as Mohawk Indians—their faces smeared with red paint and soot—rushed down to the wharf, boarded the ships, broke open 342 chests of tea—and dumped the entire contents into the harbour. It was the first act of a rebellion which was to flare into the War of Independence.

On July 4, 1776, the thirteen colonies declared themselves independent of Britain. The historic declaration came fifteen months after the first shots had been fired in the war against King George III. The war continued until 1782, and a peace treaty, a year later, formally brought it to an end. With the signing of the peace treaty, the free United States of America was born.

Americans today mark this vital period in their history by celebrating Independence Day on July 4 each year.

Had you been there in those eighteenth-century days and toured the thirteen colonies, you would have noticed a strange variety of flags. Practically every settlement had its own. Some had a design of a green fir-tree on a white ground. Others had anchor designs; still others featured the fir-tree with a coiled serpent at its foot.

The Grand Union flag—the flag that Americans now call

Geography and Climate

The United States is the nearest thing to an instant geography lesson that the world can offer. Every type of land is to be found in a country that measures 1,600 miles (over 2,500 kilometres) from north to south and 2,800 miles (over 4,500 kilometres) from east to west. There are forests, deserts, mountains, high flat lands, fertile fields, and almost every type of climate, in the United States.

The distance across America from east to west is nearly the same as that from Britain to America across the Atlantic Ocean. A fast train travelling at a steady sixty miles (over ninety-six kilometres) an hour from east to west would take two days and nights to make the journey. A fast jet plane takes five hours for the same trip.

If you were to take this plane from an airport on the Atlantic, or east, coast and fly to the Pacific, or west, coast, you would first fly over the gentle slopes of the Appalachian Mountains. Then you would fly over the rich farmlands of the Middle

Because of its size, the North American continent contains many types of climate. These cacti in the Arizona desert are the product of a hot dry climate

West. If you looked northwards, you would perhaps see the five Great Lakes lying between the United States and Canada. Speeding west, the plane would fly over vast prairies and rough cattle-grazing ground, until the snow-capped Rocky Mountains appeared. Once over this high range, the plane would glide down towards the rich valleys of California and the beaches of the Pacific Ocean.

Because of the immense size of the country and the vast distances from coast to coast, the United States has four different basic time-zones: Eastern, Central, Mountain and Pacific. When it is noon in New York, which is on Eastern time, it is an hour earlier—11 a.m.—in Chicago, on Central time; 10 a.m. in Salt Lake City, on Mountain time; and only 9 a.m. in Los Angeles, which is on Pacific time. In the two youngest states of the United States the times are different again because they lie even farther west. In both Hawaii and Alaska, it is ten hours earlier than in New York. There, it would be only 2 a.m. when it is noon in New York.

In the United States can be found every possible kind of climate, from warm, temperate zones to frozen lands. The deep green mountain forests of the north-west coast receive more than twenty times as much rain in a year as the desert lands of the south-west.

A more moderate climate has produced good farming country. This is a typical farm in Pennsylvania

A traveller from almost any part of the world will find in the U.S.A. an area that can match anything he will meet at home. He can find cool pine forests dotted with lakes or mountains covered with snow; he can find meadows with brooks and trees or wide grassy plains; broad vineyards or sandy beaches shimmering in tropical sunlight.

Today roads and railways cover the land, but only a few generations ago the mountains and plains represented great dangers for travellers. Visitors driving through the Cascade Mountains, in the western states of Oregon and Washington, can still see the marks made in the rocks by the ropes of the early settlers; for it was over these rocks that the first pioneers lowered their horses and wagons down cliffs to reach the river far below.

At another place, in the Sierra Nevada Mountains in the state of California, the main road now runs through a mountain pass which was once too narrow for a wagon to go through. Families travelling along the route in those days had to take their wagons apart piece by piece, carry them through the pass, and then reassemble them on the other side.

In the southern part of the Great Plains there is an area so flat and featureless that the first travellers drove stakes into the ground to mark the way for those to follow. Even today this area is called the "Staked Plains". Other travellers in the western valleys dropped mustard seeds on the ground, hoping that the seeds would grow into a bright yellow trail of plants to lead them out again.

In a way, much of the geography and history of the United States was determined between 10,000 and 25,000 years ago. At that time the great northern ice-cap flowed over the North American continent and its passage ground out a number of major changes in the terrain. These changes have affected everybody who has lived there since. The passage of those ice-floes determined the size and the position of the Great Lakes which stretch for 1,000 miles (1,609 kilometres) and are shared by the United States and Canada. The ice-floes changed the direction of the Missouri river and carved the channel of the Hudson river. They pushed soil off a large area of Canada into what is now the United States, creating the northern part of the Central Agricultural Basin—one of the richest farming areas in the world.

Usually one thinks of geographical boundaries in terms of mountain ranges or expanses of water. One of the most important boundaries in the United States, however, is the 20-inch (approximately 50-centimetre) rainfall line which runs from north to south, almost through the middle of the country. East of this line, farming is relatively easy and the population is consequently larger. West of the line, we find dry cattle-farming, or, if crops are grown, man-made watering systems.

When the early voyagers approached the land that is now the United States, they noticed a sweet and surprising "land smell" which told them they were near the shore. It came from the great forests which covered all the eastern parts of the country. No one knows why the forest areas ended where they

25

In the dry areas west of the rain- fall line, cattle- farming takes the place of crop-growing

did, giving way to the tall grass of the prairies—the wide, tree-less plains. The explanation remains a mystery. But it is obvious why the tall grass becomes short farther west. The reason is clearly the lack of rainfall. The line where the grass changes roughly follows the important 20-inch (50-centimetre) rainfall line.

Perhaps the greatest natural wonder in the whole of the United States is the plant-growth on the north-west coast where the mountains catch the heavy Pacific rains. Here you find forests of huge sequoia and fir-trees. Some of these great trees—often called the redwoods—are 3,000 years old—among the oldest living things known to man. These giants have such huge trunks that in one or two an archway has been cut through the trunk so that a car can be driven through the living tree. Some of these trees were seedlings when Troy fell. They were already forest giants when Rome was built. The silent forests are filled with columns of great tree-trunks lit dimly by the rays of the sun filtering through leaves far above.

26

Washington, the Capital City

The city of Washington, the capital of the United States, was specially created to be the seat of the American Government. Before a single brick was laid, the overall design for the placing of the main buildings had been decided.

George Washington, the first President of the United States, chose the site for the city in 1791, and engaged the famous French engineer Major Pierre Charles L'Enfant to draw up plans for the city.

At this time the ground was a swamp. The only people who came there were a few Scottish trappers, who camped on the banks of the Potomac river, and a few Indian tribes who hunted the area.

Yet out of this semi-wilderness, L'Enfant was able to visualise a city with wide streets running from north to south and east to west to form regular squares. Then he added diagonal avenues to criss-cross the whole area. His pattern for the ideal city survives today. In springtime, when the pink and white cherry blossom is out, it looks particularly beautiful.

Washington has perhaps the most rapidly changing population of any city in the U.S.A. It has no industrial area. One-

27

Washington, the city designed by Pierre Charles L'Enfant in 1791.
The Potomac river can be seen in the top left-hand corner of the
picture

The Supreme Court, Washington

Chief Justice of the United States administers the oath of office to the new President.

The American President, besides being the head of State, is also the head of the Government.

The American parliament is known as Congress and consists of two houses: The Senate and the House of Representatives. The members of both are elected by the voters in their states. Each member of the Senate, known as a Senator, serves for a period of six years. The members of the House of Representatives are elected every second year by all the voters in their State.

New York, the Tallest City in the World

While Washington is the political and administrative centre of the United States, New York is the centre of the commercial and business world.

If there is one thing which has made New York City famous it is the fact that it is the world's tallest city; for the small island of Manhattan in the Hudson river, which is the heart of New York, is crowded with the highest buildings known to man. Because the island is so small, the city had to grow upwards instead of outwards: it became tall instead of fat. It is an awe-inspiring experience just to walk down a New York street; the buildings, rising sheer into the blue sky on either side, make you feel as though you were walking through a deep canyon.

The oldest skyscraper in New York is the Flat Iron building, which stands at the crossroads of Broadway and Fifth Avenue. It was given this strange name because of its triangular shape, which reminded people of a heavy tailor's iron. When it was built, in 1902, it was the wonder of the Western world, for few people had ever heard of a building of 21 storeys.

Today the tallest skyscraper of all is the Empire State building, erected in 1931. It has 102 storeys, and is 1,250 feet (381

32

metres) tall. A television tower, on the roof, adds still more height.

Non-stop express lifts take just over a minute to reach the 102nd floor; but if you want to stop off at, say, the 98th floor, you take an express to the 90th floor, then change to a "local" that stops at every "station" on the way up. From the roof you can see for a distance of up to 50 miles (80 kilometres) on a clear day.

The Empire State never closes. Every hour of the day or night guides are there to answer questions or give talks on this building which dwarfs all its skyline neighbours.

Much smaller—a mere 39 storeys—is the beautiful rectangular glass and steel structure of the United Nations building. Technically, the U.N. building is not in the U.S.A. It is under the control of the United Nations, with its own police force, its own postage stamps, and even a souvenir shop selling gifts from every part of the world.

In spite of the fact that New York is the world's busiest port, and an important financial centre, it ranks as only the fourth largest city in the world in terms of population, coming after Tokio, Shanghai and London.

This is partly because, of its day-time working population of 7,781,000, one in seven lives in another city or town and commutes.

New York's story started as the result of one of the cheapest bargains in American history. In 1626, Dutch settlers gave the Indians sixty Dutch guilders for Manhattan island. If it were to be bought today it would cost one thousand million times as much.

The Indians called the island *Man-a-hat-a* which means "Heavenly Land". When the Dutch settled there they called their first settlement New Amsterdam. In 1664, however, the British sent a fleet of warships to lay siege to the island and the Dutch Governor surrendered without a fight. The settlement was re-named New York in honour of the Duke of York, who later became King James II.

New York (which is *not* the capital of the U.S.A.) is probably one of the easiest cities in which to wander around without fear of getting lost, for all the avenues run from north to south, and all the numbered streets run from east to west. The longest street is Broadway which cuts diagonally across the city.

Half-way down Broadway is Times Square—often called the crossroads of the world. One of its most fascinating features is the rich variety of moving, twisting neon signs that fill every inch of space and cover dozens of hoardings. Many of these, like cartoon strips, take minutes to tell their story.

Although Broadway is perhaps the most famous New York street, Fifth Avenue is much more beautiful. It stretches for seven miles (over ten kilometres) through the heart of the city. Here are elegant shops and beautiful hotels, fine museums and churches. There is even an outdoor ice-skating rink, open summer and winter, which is set right in the midst of the skyscrapers.

Bordering Fifth Avenue is Central Park, a large open space

Central Park, where New Yorkers come to relax and enjoy them-selves away from the bustle of their busy city

where New Yorkers come to walk, or perhaps to visit the Zoo. Central Park also contains a skating rink and two boating lakes. It is a place where people can relax and escape from the noise and bustle of the busy city.

There is one part of New York which many visitors to the city never see as it really is. This is Harlem, where many Negroes live.

35

A bird's-eye view of New York skyscrapers,
showing the outdoor skating rink nestling in
their midst

Most people visit Harlem in order to enjoy its gay clubs and
entertainment centres. In reality, it is a jungle of poverty. Its
old and crumbling buildings, overcrowded schools and dirty
streets show up clearly one of America's most urgent problems
—the unhappy position of the Negro.

Rivers

Before aeroplanes shrank the great distances of the United States, early settlers had to travel the hard way—on horseback or by canoe. There were no roads or railways. Today, the country is criss-crossed by the best road-system in the world and by magnificent railways. Even the rivers have been harnessed to help man.

There are six great rivers in the United States—the Mississippi, the Missouri, the Ohio, the Columbia, the Colorado and the Rio Grande.

The waters of the Mississippi are gathered from two-thirds of the United States. Together with the Missouri river, its chief western branch, the Mississippi flows some 4,000 miles (over 6,400 kilometres) from its northern sources in the Rocky Mountains to the Gulf of Mexico.

It is one of the longest watercourses in the world and is sometimes called "the father of waters". For many miles, it wanders along, apparently lazy and harmless. But people who know the Mississippi are not deceived by this. Americans have had many bitter struggles with Mississippi floods, and they have now managed to control the river. But they have had to work patiently at it, saving and rebuilding soil, grasslands and forests far back where the waters begin to gather. Without

37

The Mississippi,
one of America's
great rivers,
known as "the
father of waters"

such work there could have been no hope of taming the Mississippi.

Where the untamed Missouri river pours into the Mississippi from the west, it colours the river deep brown. Farther down, the waters of the Ohio river join the Mississippi. At first, the waters of the two rivers flow side by side, without mixing. Those from the west are brown; they have robbed the land of soil in areas where few plants grow. The waters from the east are clear and blue; they come from hills and valleys where plentiful forests and plant-growth have kept the soil from being washed away.

Like the Mississippi, all the waters east of the Rocky Mountains finally reach the Atlantic; all the waters to the west of the Rockies finally arrive at the Pacific. For this reason the Rocky Mountains are known as the Continental Divide. There are

38

many places in the Rockies where a visitor may throw two snowballs in opposite directions and know that each will end in a different ocean.

The two great rivers of the Pacific side are the Colorado and the Columbia. The Colorado runs through the south; the Columbia rises in Canada and flows through the north. In the dry western country, both rivers are important and necessary sources of life. They are, however, very different from one another. The Columbia used to be a swift and untamed river in pre-historic times, when its strength and force cut and shaped the land. Now it is no longer wild but flows with quiet dignity. But the Colorado is still a river of enormous fury. It rages and plunges, cutting deeply into the desert rocks. For long stretches it is impossible to cross. In spite of this, engineers have built dams on the Colorado and its swift-flowing waters have been put to work. All the farms and cities in the south-western corner of the country depend on it.

The Rio Grande, nearly 2,000 miles (3,200 kilometres) long, is the foremost river of the south-west. It forms a natural boundary between Mexico and the United States. The

A view of the
Colorado in the
state of Wyoming

Shipping entering a lock on the St Lawrence Seaway. This man-made waterway now links Canada with the heart of the United States

governments of these two countries have built irrigation and flood-control projects that benefit both.

These are nothing, however, in comparison with another man-made water project: the St Lawrence Seaway, which has opened the world's largest inland waterway—the Great Lakes —to ocean-going vessels.

Canada and the United States planned this project jointly in 1954. The Seaway was opened five years later. It allows ships to sail inland from the Atlantic Ocean. Now eighty per cent of the world's cargo ships can sail as far west as Lake Superior.

40

Railways and Roads

The United States was still being explored and settled at the time when the steam-train was first introduced, and the development of the American railways is linked for ever with the development of the country itself.

Often, in those early days, the men working on the tracks faced conditions of extreme danger. Marauding bands of Indians would harry the engineers trying to link the Atlantic with the Pacific by rail.

Yet the rise of the railway system has been quite astonishing. In 1830 there were only 23 miles (about 37 kilometres) of track in the whole of the U.S.A. By 1887 there were 157,000 miles (252,666 kilometres) of track.

Today, of course, the railways (which are all privately owned) reach even the remotest areas.

So, too, do the roads—and the Americans are justly proud of them, for they are, without doubt, the finest in the world. Great broad highways now connect most American cities. More than ninety per cent of all cities are linked with each other by wide, modern roads; and, as a result, fast motor-coach travel has become a highly profitable industry. The long-distance Greyhound buses take little longer than a train—but the fares are considerably lower.

41

An example of America's complicated but efficient road systems.
The many different road levels ensure that traffic flows smoothly

It was the birth of the mass-produced motor-car that brought the great roads to America. Now the roads have brought other industries, some of which are not found in any other part of the world. One development is the outdoor cinema. In these drive-in cinemas, which are usually located outside the towns, off the highway, the audience watch the film from their cars and pick up the sound from a portable loudspeaker handed to the driver as he buys the tickets at the main gate.

Another thriving industry which has developed from the American road-system is that of the motel. This is a hotel specially designed for motorists. The motel is made up of rows of cabins, each with parking space for the traveller's car in front of his own quarters. Every cabin has a bedroom and a bathroom; many have television and air-conditioning. Some have kitchens. Restaurants and swimming-pools are available at the larger motels.

So rapidly has this industry grown that there are now dozens of motels off every major highway in America, and travellers spend more money in them than in hotels.

The motel industry is spreading to other countries, but they still have a long way to go before they catch up with America.

A modern American motel

Mountains and Deserts

In the early days, the mountains and deserts of America were simply regions through which the settlers hurried on their way west, in search of land or gold. Then gold was found in the Rockies, men hurried back to this region, and civilisation began to reach the mountains.

The Rocky Mountains stretch all the way from Mexico to the Arctic. Like the Alps, they are high, sharp, rough and uneven. Their bare rock is capped with snow even in the south.

More than one hundred million years ago, the earth was violently folded and compressed where the Rockies now stand. Melted rock was forced up, carrying with it gold, copper, lead, silver and other metals.

The first white men to visit the mountains were the Spaniards, moving across the southern ranges to the Pacific. Stories of gold brought them here, but they did not stay in the mountains.

Not much more than a hundred years ago, the Rockies seemed almost impossible to cross; but the thought of finding gold spurred men on to do impossible things. After 1848, when gold was found in the river beds of California, great numbers of people crossed the mountains and deserts, over trails discovered by the early mountaineers. Today, eight railways and

The Rocky Mountains were once thought impassable. Today, they can be crossed by rail or road

a dozen major roads go winding over the mountains. They follow the same routes established by the early settlers.

Back in those days, thousands of men settled in this wilderness, and agriculture began to come to the Rockies. Farmers raised food to sell to settlers on their way to the west. Most farmers were Mormons, members of a religious group, who were seeking some hidden valley in the mountains, some land that no one else would want. They discovered the Great Salt Lake where they settled, and founded Salt Lake City.

In this land of little fresh water, agriculture was very difficult.

45

It would have been impossible if farmers had not planned and worked together. Fearing nothing, they built more than one hundred towns in an area which other men had considered worthless. Water, carefully brought by canal, made their land productive.

Below the mountains were equally inhospitable stretches of land: the deserts. Three generations ago, the desert wasteland stretched from the Mississippi Valley in the east almost to the Pacific coast in the west. But men learned that prairies could grow maize and that grasslands could feed cattle or yield wheat. So the size of the desert decreased.

Today there are still nearly 70,000 square miles (181,300 square kilometres) of desert in the U.S.A. Between Salt Lake City and Reno in Nevada, there is nothing to be found but dead lakes, dry rivers, snakes and small animal life—and enormous mineral wealth. Although the area is the size of an empire, its population is no bigger than that of a town.

Here, in the triangle of land between the Sierra Nevada Mountains in the west and the Rockies in the east, the climate is dry and hot. Even fairly large rivers dry up so rapidly that they vanish before they reach the end of the desert.

In southern California—which is usually thought of as fertile country—more than 2,000 square miles (5,180 square kilometres) west of the Colorado River is still desert. This includes Death Valley near the Nevada border. It was named in 1849 after a group of pioneers first crossed the territory. The valley is actually a deep trough. It contains the lowest level of land in the western hemisphere, at the town of Bad Water. The land at Bad Water is 282 feet (85·95 metres) *below* sea level.

Now the American, with his engineering skills, is making more and more of the desert bloom.

One of the miracles of this desert region is the Hoover Dam on the Colorado river, which has made barren land fertile. The dam, more than 700 feet (213 metres) high, was completed in 1936. Prosperous farms nestle in its shade. The dam produces enough electricity to supply power to all the houses over

The great sand-dunes of the Colorado desert

The Hoover Dam which has transformed vast stretches of desert-land into fertile country

a vast region. It gives a flow of clean water to vast stretches of what was formerly desert. It controls the floods that formerly wiped out farm after farm. It was the start of a dream—that one day all the deserts of America would be transformed into productive land.

48

The Deep South

Few cities in the United States are as close to the past as New Orleans, facing the Gulf of Mexico and deep in America's South. Here, the influence of the French, who founded the city in the eighteenth century, is still strongly felt, as is that of the Spanish, who came to join the French, and the Negroes who had been brought over from Africa as slaves.

Since the early Colonial days, New Orleans and the South generally had believed that slavery was essential to their way of life. There had been slaves in the South for nearly two hundred years before they were freed by Lincoln, in 1865.

How did slavery arise? It started because the farmers of the South needed workers to grow their crops of cotton, rice, sugar and tobacco. As this was a new country, with a small agricultural population, there were not enough workers to go round. The Southerners therefore began to bring over Africans, to work in the fields as slaves.

The situation in the North was different from that in the South. Instead of farming, most people were involved in manufacturing, finance and commerce—all the skills which needed brains rather than brawn. The Northerners saw that this slavery was cruel and unjust, while the Southerners believed it to be an economic necessity.

Thus, the North was on the whole violently opposed to slavery, while the South continued to encourage it.

For years, agitation spread to stop slavery, but it was a

A statue of Abraham Lincoln, who gave the slaves their freedom in 1865. This is the central point of the Lincoln Memorial in Washington

simple story in a magazine that applied the match which started the blaze. In 1851, an unknown writer named Harriet Beecher Stowe wrote a magazine short story, describing the death of a slave called Uncle Tom. Mrs. Stowe had her readers weeping over the tale, which caught the imagination of the public, and so she embarked on a full-length story about Uncle Tom, the now-famous *Uncle Tom's Cabin*. Her book angered slave-owners; but stirred those who despised slavery to much greater efforts.

The head-on collision between North and South came when Abraham Lincoln stood for President in 1860 on the promise that if he was elected he would prohibit slavery. He won—and gave the slaves their freedom in 1865.

Before that, however, the South had seen what would happen if Lincoln won. They at once withdrew from the Union, formed their own union, which they called the Confederate States of America, and elected their own President. So civil war loomed. It was to be a war between the North (The Union) and the South (The Confederacy). The North won the war after five years of bitter, disastrous fighting.

Strangely enough, although the bitterest fighting was in the South, few traces of the Civil War can be seen in New Orleans. But in this beautiful city much of the earlier America remains.

So, too, does the French and Spanish heritage. The French flag was planted there in 1682 when the French explorers braved the wide brown Mississippi river and took over the whole rich area for France, naming it Louisiana in honour of the French King Louis XI.

Nearly a hundred years were to pass, however, before the country could boast a town. This they named Nouvelle Orleans in honour of the French Regent, the Duke of Orleans.

By 1740, six years after it had been founded, it had become the Versailles of the West, filled with courtly elegance and typically French in customs and manners. Then, abruptly, it

Some of the houses of New Orleans, such as this one, still show the influence of the early French settlers

passed into Spanish hands when the French King gave the whole area to his cousin the King of Spain as a present. For 40 years Spanish settlers flooded in to join the French—and a new race, the people now known as Creoles, was born.

Then New Orleans became a French possession once again —until 1803, when it became part of the biggest land-sale bargain in the history of the United States. In that year, Napoleon sold, for what now seems an absurdly small sum, all the land which the French possessed—a strip right up the centre of the United States, stretching from the Gulf of Mexico as far north as Canada. The purchase doubled the size of the American nation; later the land was divided up into 14 states.

52

The Louisiana Purchase, as the deal is called, brought hundreds of thousands of people from other countries to join this new nation.

Among the contributions which the Negroes of New Orleans made was a new form of music: jazz. Many different ingredients had gone to produce jazz—the wistful, sad songs of the Negro slaves, the work-songs and chants of the plantation workers, the rhythms of the tom-toms used in voodoo rites, even the old Negro hymns. All these were part of the musical folklore of the South when the first jazz-men took over.

To this mixture the musicians added the rollicking tunes played on combs by street urchins, the sing-song of the street peddlars, all the rhythmical sounds they heard around them. Each time a tune was played, there was scope for fresh variation. The new music caught on like a fever in the years before the First World War.

Each January, New Orleans holds its annual carnival, known as *Mardi Gras*—a time when the whole town goes mad, with a series of masked balls and dances, which recalls the early French days. The carnival goes on for ten days, reaching its climax on Shrove Tuesday when the entire population joins in the festivities.

There is music everywhere, and dancing, in fancy dress or masks, in almost every street. This custom is believed to date back to 1827 when some wealthy Creole boys, returning from their studies in Paris, decided to sing and dance in the streets as the people of France did, and still do, each Shrove Tuesday.

53

Mardi Gras, the
gayest time of
the year in New
Orleans

The city is decorated with gold, purple and green; everyone
sings the traditional Mardi Gras song:

If ever I cease to love thee,
If ever I cease to love,
May the fish get legs and the cows lay eggs,
If ever I cease to love.

The song has an odd tale behind it. A visiting nobleman
from Europe (the Grand Duke Alexis Alexandrovich Romanov)
fell in love with an American actress who was singing the ditty
in 1872. At the Grand Duke's request, every carnival band
played the tune all through Mardi Gras to remind him of his
love. It has been played every year since.

54

Crop-growing and Cattle-farming

Everyone has his or her own idea of what the Americans do for a living. Many are wrong—for Americans do other things besides producing films, motor-cars or tinned food, or putting men on the moon.

Three-fifths of the land on which they live is farmland, and more than one-seventh of the American people live on farms. And here's an interesting point: just before the Second World War, when the number of working people in the U.S. was 50 million, eighteen out of every hundred workers were farmers, and each man produced enough to feed ten others. Today, only seven out of every hundred work on the farms. Yet each man today produces enough to feed twenty-three people.

Behind these fascinating statistics lies a story of mechanical and scientific progress which has completely transformed the farming community of the United States. The tractor and the combine-harvester—both developed in the United States— have replaced the work animals and cut down back-breaking jobs. Output has been increased and workers freed from the more tedious tasks. In just over a hundred years, the average working week for the farm labourer has fallen from seventy hours to just under forty-five.

Science has developed new strains of animals and plants. Fertilisers, and chemicals to control weeds and destroy harmful insects, have increased farm-production. In addition, farming has now become linked with the great American canning industry. Modern methods of freezing, canning and packing have created opportunities for the farmer to produce more.

The heart of America's farmland lies in the great "corn belt" which stretches across the states of Indiana, Illinois, Iowa and

A fleet of combine-harvesters at work

Nebraska. Fields not of wheat but of maize ("corn" is another word for maize in America), hay or beans, stretch endlessly, until the eye tires. This area extends from the shores of Lake Superior in the north to Texas in the south, from Ohio in the east to Nebraska in the west.

It is a beautiful, varied country, blessed with rich soil. Decades ago the area was settled by Scandinavians, and today people in the corn belt are often fair-haired and bear Scandinavian names.

Farmers in the corn belt claim they can actually *hear* the corn growing. It has always been a stock joke—but, in fact, the farmers can almost *see* it grow, for in the rich soil, maize will grow two inches (five centimetres) in a single night, and by late summer will have grown to twice the height of a man. It is America's most important farming crop. Two-thirds of all farms grow some maize. Vast quantities are exported all over the world as cattle food.

The maize farmer of today uses machinery for every step in his operation. Machines plough, plant, enrich the soil, kill weeds, harvest, remove the husks, separate the grain and chop the stalks.

Today one man and his son—even where a boy is still attending school and only helps his father part of the time—can look after a huge farm, a task that before mechanisation would have taken ten or more workers.

The modern corn-belt farmer is also likely to run a herd of cattle, although the real cattle country is farther south, in the area known as the Great Plains which stretches from North Dakota in the north to Texas. The Great Plains includes all North and South Dakota, parts of Montana and Wyoming which you will find on the map to the west of Dakota, and parts of Iowa, Kansas, Oklahoma, New Mexico and Texas. The Great Plains is the real "cowboy country".

It is an area of intense heat and extreme cold, a land where, in some places, water is worth more than property. It is almost completely flat for 400 miles (650 kilometres) until it suddenly meets the mountains of the west. The wind blows continuously and the weather is very hot from July to September, but in most winters there are heavy snowfalls which often bury barns and farmhouses to roof level.

Most of the men who first came to this region were merely passing through on their way to the Pacific Coast valleys. But some who came stayed. They were attracted by the countless bison and cattle which they saw roaming the vast pasture-lands; and they dreamed of a time when this cattle might supply the eastern cities with food and leather.

The thousands of wild cattle which they found grazing on the rich prairie-grass were descended from six young cows and a bull that had come from Mexico with the Spaniards in 1521. By 1870, vast herds of cattle were there for the taking. A man needed only horses, some supplies and a few helpers to gather in wild animals. The legend of the Wild West cowboy had begun.

Soon, meat-packing companies were established in Chicago.

The fierce cattle with long horns were scattered over very wide areas. They had to be rounded up by cowboys and driven in herds across the plains. The cowboys had to be tough; they would have to fight bands of thieves, weather fierce storms, ford flooded rivers or face angry farmers whose crops had been crushed by the driven herds. Indians, too, fought them or demanded payment from cattlemen crossing their lands.

The drives were long and slow. A herd might travel 15 miles (24 kilometres) a day, but at night the nervous cattle had to be calmed and rested. To keep them quiet, cowboys rode circling about the herd throughout the night, singing to the animals. This was part of the cowboy's work; and his sad, slow songs have become part of the American folk art.

This man and his horse bring to mind the exciting legends of the Wild West, in which the cowboy was king

Within a few years, herds of heavy cattle moving eastwards had made deep trails. The trails led to towns such as Dodge City, called "cow towns" because their trade consisted mainly in handling, buying and selling cattle. The rough, noisy towns were part of the true Wild West.

Gradually, the herds increased and the cattlemen turned to the northern plains. As the bison died and the Indians left, a vast ocean of grass became open for cattle feeding.

Then a man near Chicago discovered a method of shipping fresh meat over long distances in ice-cooled railway wagons. It was the beginning of the end for the Wild West.

Today the Great Plains are ruled by a new cattle industry. Co-operative groups have been formed; the groups divide the land among the farmer members and decide how many cattle should graze on each piece. Scientific experts have been brought in to study the land and the grass, and as a result of their findings local regulations have been introduced. New life has been given to the area.

Science has also improved the quality of the cattle. After years of experimenting, the largest ranch-owners have succeeded in crossing Brahma cattle from India with the heavy American type. The Indian Brahma has passed on to the American beast the advantage of being able to endure the heat, while the American cattle still retains its fine beef quality.

The Vanishing Indians

Today, there are about 400,000 Indians scattered across the United States. This is a tiny proportion of the total population. There would have been many more if they had not been almost wiped out during the early savage fighting as the settlers pushed westwards.

One of the great tragedies of early American history is the manner in which thousands of these fine and noble people were slaughtered. It is easy to understand that the promise of riches in those days attracted bad as well as good men. Greed was so strong in some that they thought nothing of wiping out whole bands of Indians. The Indians attacked in their turn. And so the number of casualties increased.

Gradually the Indians were driven to the Far West, and it was there that they settled in the hope that they would be allowed this last free home. During the thirty years before 1890, however, they found even this vanishing as the new Americans opened up Nebraska and Kansas. In the search for land, Indian reservations—land which they had been guaranteed would be theirs for ever—were threatened or stolen outright by unscrupulous land dealers.

One can understand how easy it was to do this. There were

no laws for people to abide by. If a man was powerful enough, he made his own. And more often than not there was no one to whom honest men and women could turn for help.

By the 1860s, known as the "roaring sixties", things had got to such a pitch that the Indians started launching raids on the white "invaders". The Sioux tribe always seemed to be in the forefront of the fighting. It was the Sioux who, after their land had been stolen, raided what is now Minnesota and massacred hundreds of white settlers. The whites were quick to revenge their fallen comrades and the women and children who had

62

been murdered in their covered wagons. But they could not always tell friend from enemy. As fighting flared up along what is now the Colorado border, the whites killed hundreds of friendly Indians. War swept the whole area.

The American people were divided. The moderate members of the government wanted to pacify the tribes and give them enough land to make them contented. The army, on the other hand, wanted to crush them; they felt that this was the only safe way to bring order to the swiftly growing country. The army got its way. The result was a series of violent skirmishes and battles all along the border-country. The Apaches held out until 1868, before being defeated by the army.

The hostile Sioux, however, kept fighting until 1876, when the army mounted an expedition against them and their famous chief, Sitting Bull. This legendary battle was one of the most fierce ever fought in Indian territory. More than two hundred white men were killed before the Sioux gave in. Even so, they rose again fourteen years later, but this time the slaughter of the proud tribe was so savage that the Sioux never fought again.

There is another aspect to this tragedy, for it now seems fairly certain that before the white man came the Indians were for the most part peaceful. It was only the white men who turned them into warriors and gave us the picture we have today—so often portrayed in the films of Cowboys and Indians —of bloodthirsty savages.

People who have studied the American Indians and their history say that there would be little crime in the United States

As these Pueblo Indians perform a traditional war dance they are perhaps remembering the time when they fought for their land

if everyone followed the peaceful Indian laws. Before the white man came to America, dishonesty was unknown. But when the white man sold the Indians rifles he also taught them their worst habits.

Now, however, the white man is trying to repair some of the damage done in the past. Special laws have been passed which make it a crime to steal Indian lands. Indian children can go to their own schools, and Indians in the two hundred-odd tribes which survive are being encouraged to hold their own ancient ceremonies, while some of the land previously stolen from them is being given back.

Most Indians live on reservations. There is no suggestion that they are prisoners on these large tracts of land where they live. They are free and can go where they like. But the Indians do not fit in with the hurly-burly of twentieth-century machine-age America, and so the reservations are there to help them, to enable them to lead their own way of life.

Although in a way the present state of the once-proud Indians is sad and pathetic, there are many famous Americans today who are proud to boast that they have Indian blood in them.

Quite often as you travel along the fast modern motorways that straddle the United States—many running across lands where the Indians used to roam—you will see signboards announcing "Indian Trading Post". The stalls or small stores are filled with gaily coloured blankets, strings of beads, bows and arrows, tomahawks, knives and moccasins. The grave Indian—a feather in his jet black hair—will try to sell you a souvenir and boast that all his stock is the work of Indians living in nearby reservations.

More likely than not, however, the goods will turn out to be fakes, mass-produced in factories and sold to small stores owned by white men without a drop of Indian blood in their veins. The shopkeeper hires a local Indian to make the place look authentic and more exciting for the tourists.

Taming the Wild West

The Wild West, as it is pictured in the cinema, has changed. It has been tamed. It is true that in Texas—whose people are so independent that it is called the "lone star state"—you can still see cowboys in ten-gallon hats. But this state, which is typical of the West, has changed more than any in the whole of the United States.

A man living there today is far more likely to be a worker in an oil-field, or a scientist, than a cattle-drover. But even so he will probably still wear a cowboy hat and boots, for the Texans have clung to their old style of dressing.

What has led the state away from its farming and cattle-breeding past? One single event: the discovery, in 1901, of oil near Beaumont, not far from the Gulf of Mexico.

This proved to be the turning-point in the future of Texas. From this moment, the search for oil dominated everything else. The climax of the search came with the great oil discovery of 1930, when drillers found the famous East Texas oil-field. This is the largest oil-field in the world, and now has more than 19,000 wells working to produce oil.

Although oil is now the lifeblood of Texas, the state is still changing. It has entered the Space Age. At Houston, the Government has set up its Manned Spacecraft Centre, the

66

Oil-wells in Kilgore, a boom town in Texas

headquarters of all manned space projects. The Centre employs some 3,500 people.

With the development of Houston as a space centre, many allied industries have moved in. Private firms making equipment, laboratories engaged on space research, university departments dealing with space medicine—all are new to the city where, not so many years ago, cattle thieves used to operate.

Today, there are more than 250,000 men and women concerned with space in Texas, and to house them an entirely new town called Clear Lake City is being built. When it is finished, in the late 1970s, it will give work to an additional 70,000 people.

San Francisco in California is another city that has changed with the times. In 1848, it had 800 inhabitants. Then came the dramatic news that gold had been discovered at Sutter's Mill, 100 miles (160 kilometres) to the north-east. Within two weeks the population of San Francisco had dropped—to seven!

San Francisco, with the harbour in the background

By the beginning of the following year, however, San Francisco was booming. This city, built on hills and with a magnificent harbour, was the place to which the gold-miners swarmed when they had "struck it rich". It became a city of tents and shacks filled with "gold-men", as they were called. Ships from every part of the world were abandoned in the harbour as the crews deserted to seek gold.

The city was one of the wildest in the Wild West. The Barbary Coast—as the district round the waterfront was called —became the centre of crime that often went unpunished. Fires broke out repeatedly in the wooden shacks—started deliberately to make robbery easier.

Oddly enough, as the gold-fever died, San Francisco's prosperity grew. Fortunes made in the gold-rush brought culture to this beautiful city—many say the most beautiful in the United States. Large houses sprang up on Nob Hill—so called because that was where "the nobs" lived—which is now the city's hotel district.

The city grew even larger after 1859 when the building of the transcontinental railway was completed. This railway had a curious effect on the population of San Francisco. Thousands of Chinese had worked their way across America building the railway. When it was finished, they settled there, with the result that today San Francisco has the largest Chinese settlement outside Asia. Here, more than 25,000 people live in their own district, known as Chinatown. Their houses are Oriental in style; they wear Chinese clothes. Their shops are filled with Chinese furniture, porcelain and toys and with strange, exotic foods.

San Francisco's Chinatown. Even the lamp-posts have an Oriental air

Industry and Engineering

The United States is the undisputed industrial giant of the twentieth century. Names like Chicago, Detroit and Los Angeles are household words in almost every country of the world.

The fact that these major cities are separated from one another by vast distances means that each is different in character although all are hubs of the great industrial giant.

Chicago, which stretches along the shores of Lake Michigan, is the second largest city in the United States.

Called "the windy city" (because of the strong winds off the lake), Chicago believes in "bigness". It claims to have the world's largest hotel and the world's busiest airport; it even boasts the world's busiest corner—on State Street—where over a quarter of a million shoppers crowd the stores every weekday. Its sports ground at Soldier Field holds 101,000 spectators.

One odd fact about Chicago is that it has the only river in the world which flows backwards. Until 1900 the Chicago river used to flow into Lake Michigan, but engineers, fearing that pollution from the city might spoil the lake, reversed the flow!

70

Set in the middle of the corn belt, Chicago (which takes its name from the Indian word *Checagou*, meaning wild-onion place) owes its basic prosperity to grain, livestock and farm produce. At one time, the city was also the centre of the world's largest meat-packing industry. It still boasts: "We eat what we can, and can what we can't." More than five million cattle, pigs and sheep pass through the city's stockyards each year—and most of them come out again in tins!

Today, however, meat is no longer Chicago's major industry. The city is an industrial giant in its production of iron and steel.

Chicago is a comparatively new city, for the whole area was under the control of the Indians until 1794, when General "Mad Anthony" Wayne beat them in a battle at Fallen Timbers. After this battle, the Indians ceded to the United States "one piece of land six miles square at the mouth of the Chicakgo river", as the transfer document describes it. Today it covers 224 square miles (580 square kilometres).

There is one aspect of its history that the city would like to forget—a period of crime and violence in the 1920s and 1930s. In 1919, the American Government passed a law prohibiting the manufacture or sale of alcohol. In spite of the law, the sale of alcohol continued, in secret, and huge profits were made by the men who ran this illegal liquor trade.

At that time, Chicago's prosperity had attracted many rather unsavoury characters. These people formed themselves into powerful criminal gangs to exploit this illegal traffic in liquor, and competition between the rival organisations became fierce. Gang murders became common and violence reached its peak on St Valentine's Day, 1929, when a gang disguised as policemen fought a running battle with their rivals.

Detroit, one of the other industrial giants, is quite different from Chicago. Her history, as an industrial centre, can be considered to have started in 1818, when the steamship *Walk in the Water* first sailed the Great Lakes as far as Detroit, and cut the travelling time between that city and Buffalo from an average of 7 days to 44 hours. This led to the building of the Erie Canal in 1825, after which industry followed swiftly.

Today, Detroit is the world's greatest car-producing city. Since the early days of the twentieth century, Detroit has meant "cars" to the rest of the world. Much of this success was due to one man, Henry Ford, who insisted that the future of the new motor-car industry lay in making the car a necessity rather than a luxury. Ford saw that, in order to achieve this, mass-production would be needed.

Like most American cities, Detroit is a "melting-pot" of many races, and today the largest section of its community is the Polish one. Polish people flocked from Europe, lured by the high wages in the new car factories. On the west side of Detroit is a Polish Colony known as the "Hamtramck" district, which has its own municipality. Here, the restaurants, shops, drug-stores, garages and other businesses have Polish names. There are shop-signs in both Polish and English. Some of the

A Detroit car-assembly line

daily papers are printed in Polish, and there are Polish cinemas and Polish churches.

Los Angeles, a third great industrial centre, was once the chief cattle-market of the state of California, and is now to many people another name for Hollywood. In fact the cinema industry forms only a small, and diminishing, part of the city's economy. Today, aircraft and electronic equipment are the most important industries in the district. There are others: only Akron in Ohio makes more rubber tyres than Los Angeles; only Detroit makes more cars.

Now let us take a look at one of America's most remarkable engineering feats, one of the most amazing triumphs of man over nature. It is called the Tennessee Valley Authority—or the T.V.A., for short.

It stands in the mighty river regions of the Mississippi, the Ohio, the Holston and the Colorado where land had for years been wasting away. This was due not only to repeated heavy flooding, but also to soil-erosion, the early colonists having cut down all the trees and robbed the soil of its nutriment.

So a once-rich area lay bare and denuded, and by 1933 the Tennessee Valley was in danger of becoming a vast tract of wasteland.

Something had to be done; and it was. Thirty-three years of work have seen gigantic dams spring up on the Tennessee river. Another twenty-two dams now control the tributaries.

74

From the air, they look like a great flight of steps leading the river gently down its winding path. The destructive water has now become the servant of the people, and this once-barren land now flourishes again. But the water is not only being used for land-irrigation; it is also being harnessed to produce hydro-electricity, supplying power and light to the whole area.

In 1933, when the Tennessee Valley Authority came into being, foresters found that fire, flood and erosion had almost wiped out the advantages of the valley's climate. Today, more than ninety-six per cent of the valley's fifteen million forest acres are free of fire-hazards and new timber industries have created jobs for over fifty thousand people. The end of the dreaded flood-erosion has given a new lease of life to lands that had ceased to bear crops.

Today, when mountain-rivers are raging, messages flash from dam to dam along the T.V.A. A message arrives at the control room of the Hiwassee Dam: "Hold back all the water of the Hiwassee river. Keep it out of the Tennessee." To the Cherokee Dam on the Holston river the message is: "Hold back the Holston." To Chickamauga Dam on the Tennessee river itself: "Release water to make space for waters from above." Behind these messages lies a regular system of reporting rainfall and the flow of water from all over the huge basin.

The taming of the river had an additional effect which has given pleasure to millions. The dam system has created a chain of quiet water—a series of lakes with 10,000 miles (16,093 kilometres) of shoreline where people can boat, fish and camp.

The Negroes

When, in the Colonial days, and under the protection of the British Government, thousands of Negroes were imported from Africa to work as slaves, no one could have foreseen the resulting problem that was to grip the whole of the United States.

In spite of the fact that they were freed, by Abraham Lincoln in 1863, the coloured people were never allowed to forget their background and were considered as inferiors. The way in which they were treated was in direct conflict with the aims of the Declaration of Independence, drawn up on July 4, 1776. This historic document stated, in the following words, the belief that all men were created equal: "We hold these truths to be self-evident, that all men are created equal, that they are endowed by their Creator with certain unalienable rights, that among these are life, liberty and the pursuit of happiness."

Right up until the 1930s, the official policy of the United States was to separate the Negroes from the Whites, with the result that the Negroes—unlike the Indians who had their own reservations—became almost outcasts. The courts ruled that they should be segregated from Whites in schools, in places of entertainment, on trains and buses. Negro schools were noticeably inferior to those of the white people. Coloured men serving in the Forces rarely became anything but kitchen workers and labourers.

But since then the picture has changed almost daily. In the

Negro and white children now go to school together

Forces today Negroes can, and often do, become officers commanding units composed mainly of white men.

Many states rigidly enforce the laws under which a Negro can take legal action against any employer who refuses him a vacant job on the grounds of colour, race or creed.

The most striking improvement in the situation of the Negroes has been in the field of education. The courts have now ruled that separate education for white children and black is illegal.

The courts have made similar rulings covering public transport, recreation and public accommodation, so that Negroes now sit next to white people on buses and in theatres and stay in any hotel they choose.

But mere court rulings do not entirely solve the problem. Down in the deep South, there have been riots and violent demonstrations against the new laws. Most Americans recognise that a long and difficult road lies ahead before the goal of complete racial equality is reached.

A coloured skin still remains a great handicap, and it is still a fact that a Negro American has about half as much chance of completing high school, and one third as much chance of becoming a professional man, as a White American.

But things are improving. In the North, in the big cities such as New York, Chicago and Detroit, people undoubtedly look more favourably on the Negro than they did even ten years ago. Even so, it will still be some time before the Americans can honestly say: "We've got the problem licked".

Reaching for the Sky

The United States shares with Russia a desire to explore all the possibilities of progress in the Space Age. Both nations are interested in developing space travel and in exploring outer space.

Vast sums are spent on projects, such as that of sending men to the moon, which only a few years ago would have seemed like science-fiction. It is all coming true.

Because of the vast distances which people have to travel in the United States, America has always been interested in finding more efficient ways of shrinking the distances. And it is only a short step from aeroplanes to rockets.

It all started with two American brothers named Orville and Wilbur Wright. The Wright brothers had been fascinated by the possibility of flying ever since they had first experimented with gliders, and found they could stay in the air for more than a minute.

In 1903, they made a small petrol engine to power their glider, but the first flight was a failure. The engine stalled and the plane settled gently on the ground.

The second flight, however, lasted for 12 seconds and the plane travelled 120 feet (36·376 metres). In those few moments, the American aviation industry was born.

The Wright brothers organised a flying team to demonstrate their planes, but it was only after the First World War that the aircraft industry really began to grow; then commercial air-lines started crossing the continent.

Charles A. Lindbergh was, perhaps, the most famous of American pioneer fliers. On May 20, 1927, he flew alone non-stop from New York to Paris in a plane little larger than the first plane of the Wright brothers. Man was on his way to conquering the skies. Soon, Americans were to reach even higher—into outer space.

The key-point in the U.S. space programme is at Cape

The Vehicle Assembly Building at Cape Kennedy from which moon rockets are launched. In the foreground are the mobile launch plat-forms where space vehicles are assembled for transportation to the launching-pad

The main firing-line at Cape Kennedy. The mushroom-shaped block-houses can be seen on the right of the picture

Kennedy on the east coast of Florida. It is here that the rockets are launched.

Looking down on Cape Kennedy from the air, it is possible to see just how vast the buildings are which hold the space vehicles—some are the size of 40 football pitches put together.

A huge blister-like building of concrete, looking rather like a fully opened mushroom, houses the launch-control centre. It is designed so that if a vehicle should explode during launching, no one inside the "mushroom" would be harmed. Here a mass of computer-controlled machines count the seconds to "blast-off", measure the rocket's electronic control-system and record every moment outside. Television cameras and peri-scopes link the centre with the rocket on the pad.

Cape Kennedy is really a city quite different from any other in the U.S.A. Here, people's lives and their work are con-centrated on one thing: space.

81

The Two New States

In 1959 two vastly different regions, and very far apart, officially joined the Union. They are Alaska, which became the forty-ninth state, and Hawaii, which became the fiftieth. Both had been linked politically with the U.S. for a long time.

Alaska, which joined the Union just before Hawaii, is the largest state in America. Yet since it was first purchased from the Russians in 1867 little interest had been shown in it. It was a country of icebergs and polar bears situated beyond Canada's western borders. It was too far from the settled areas of the United States.

In those parts of Alaska that lie above the Arctic Circle, it is still a land of bears and icebergs. The land there is frozen to a considerable depth. Although from May until August the sun never sets on this flat, treeless region it never manages to melt the earth to a depth of more than a yard.

In spite of being the largest state, only 250,000 people live

Eskimo citizens of Alaska

there, including some thousands of Eskimoes. Of the huge areas of its land which are fit for cultivation, less than one per cent is actually cultivated.

The Japan Current of the Pacific warms some of the southeast part of Alaska, while the whole of the north and west is enclosed by icy Arctic waters. This means that the climate is variable. Temperatures fall far below zero in some parts and rise as high as 86°F (30°C) in other parts. In a year, more than 450 inches (over 1,000 centimetres) of snow may fall in the north, while 86 inches (nearly 220 centimetres) of rain falls on the capital city of Juneau in the south.

There are only about 5,000 miles (8,000 kilometres) of roads and 600 miles (965 kilometres) of railways in the whole of Alaska, although almost every town has its own airfield.

The chief source of income, and the industry which has contributed most to Alaska's economic progress, is her fisheries. Salmon, cod, halibut, crab and shrimp are some of the fish which are caught in her teeming waters. After fishing, the state's biggest industry is lumber and wood-pulp. There are also large deposits of coal, copper and other important minerals.

At one time, there were deposits of gold, also. In 1898, gold was first discovered in Anvil Creek. This discovery brought a rush of people to the area and the town of Nome was born.

Juneau, the capital of Alaska. Because the city is hemmed in by two massive mountains, it is long and narrow, and its streets wind up the steep slopes

The very first log cabin built in Alaska still stands in Nome—a town less than a hundred years old.

The roaring days of the gold-rush brought 20,000 people to Nome. Now, fewer than 3,000 people live there.

Nome, slightly south of the Arctic circle, is the southernmost Eskimo city, and the largest one in the Alaskan Arctic. Only 165 miles (just over 265 kilometres) away is Siberia, in the U.S.S.R.

The beaches of Nome are sprinkled with gold, but the only people who show any interest in it are the visitors. Anyone can try his hand at panning, but after a hard day's work sifting through great quantities of sand he will be lucky if he has found enough to buy him dinner that evening. There is no longer any commercial gold-mining in the area—the yield is too low to make it worth while.

In the summer, the country around Nome is covered in grass and wild flowers, even though just a little way down the earth has actually turned into permafrost—ground that has been frozen for longer than can be recorded.

During the summer months, Nome is a scene of great activity as the King Island Eskimoes arrive in their walrus-skin boats from their homes in the Bering Sea. They come to sell the ivory which they have carved out of walrus teeth and tusks.

Just seventy-one years after the gold-miners pushed their dog sleds across Alaska's icy slopes, a new breed of adventurer has started to "invade" this vast land.

Two United States oil companies found, almost by chance,

a pair of wells which suggested that beneath the frozen waste was one of the richest oil fields in the world. Soon petrol companies of the world were bidding for land from Alberta to the McKenzie River delta, along Alaska's northern slopes and then again north into the Arctic seas.

Even now no one can tell how much oil is there, but the most conservative estimates suggest that output will run into thousands of millions of barrels a year.

Alaska will never be the same again. Until the discovery of oil, it was a region with few modern conveniences and poor communications, an area of vast ice-clad wastelands. Now the oil companies of the world are pouring in money for roads, medical facilities and schools. Alaska will never be warm—but the growing number of inhabitants will be able to be cold in comfort.

How different Alaska is from Hawaii, the youngest state in America!

Hawaii is actually a chain of twenty islands in the Pacific. It is the only state in the U.S.A. which does not lie on the mainland of North America. In fact, the nearest state—California—is 2,000 miles (3,218 kilometres) away.

The largest island, which is also called Hawaii, lies at the south-eastern end of the chain and is almost twice as large as all the other islands combined.

The islands are fortunate in having rich volcanic soil. This has been made fertile through scientific agriculture and man-made waterways. Although there are no fuel resources and few useful minerals except sulphur, there are many industries. Honolulu alone manufactures more than 160 different products.

No one even knew of the existence of the islands until 1778. In January of that year, Captain James Cook of the British Navy landed on one of the islands. He was welcomed by the Hawaiians who treated him well. He named his discovery the Sandwich Islands in honour of the Earl of Sandwich, the First Lord of the Admiralty.

Cook stayed two weeks on his first visit and returned later to establish trading posts. He was killed by the natives on his third visit in 1779 when a quarrel broke out between them and his sailors.

The islands were ruled by native chiefs until 1800 when the

Hawaii, the youngest state in America, attracts large numbers of tourists each year. Here are some of them enjoying a display of Hawaiian dancing

whole chain was united under a Hawaiian king. They became a republic in 1894, a possession of the U.S.A. in 1898, a U.S. "territory" in 1900, and a state in 1959.

With their beautiful beaches and pleasant climate, the islands of Hawaii now have a flourishing tourist trade. But their main income is not derived from this; it comes from two major crops: pineapples and sugar.

Hawaii is the world's chief source of pineapples. Indeed, one whole island—Lanai—is owned by a single company, solely for the purpose of growing pineapples. Every inch of cultivated land on the island is given over to pineapples, and there is only one settlement there, Lanai city.

But more important even than pineapples is sugar. About one-third of all the sugar produced on American soil is produced in Hawaii.

These young Americans have come from a nearby summer-camp for an afternoon's boating

America—those who are old enough—take some sort of job after the school day is over, as well as during the holidays. It is an American tradition for young students to work in order to earn money for their entertainment, clothes and school expenses.

They have no objection to taking whatever jobs they can find—as waiters, shop assistants, office boys, petrol-station attendants, farm hands or labourers, or they may earn money delivering newspapers.

The number of hours they are allowed to work is controlled by law. But the work does, in fact, provide many boys and girls with a lot of fun, as well as pocket-money. Hundreds every year accept work in the cafeterias and motels of some of America's magnificent national parks, and so not only earn money but also learn something of their great country.

Index

Alaska 23, 82–6
Anvil Creek 84
Apache Indians 63
Appalachian Mountains 21

Bad Water 47
Barbary Coast 68
baseball 89–91
Boston 9
Boston Tea Party 17, 18
Broadway 32, 34

Cape Kennedy 80, 81
Capitol 30
Cascade Mountains 24
Central Park 34, 35
Chicago 14, 59, 60, 70, 71, 72
Chinese 69
Civil War 50, 51
Clear Lake City 67
Colorado River 37, 39, 47, 48, 74

Columbia 37, 38
colonies 16
Columbus, Christopher 13, 16
Congress 31
Continental Divide 38
Cook, James 87
Corn Belt 57
cowboys 59, 60
Creoles 52, 53

Death Valley 46, 47
Declaration of Independence 76
Department of Defence 29
deserts 46
Detroit 72

Empire State Building 30, 32, 33
Ericson, Leif 16
Eskimoes 83, 85

farming 55, 56, 57, 58
Fifth Avenue 34

first settlements 16, 17
Fiftieth State 82
Flat Iron Building 32
football 89
forests 25
Forty-ninth State 82

George III, King 17, 18
gold 67, 68
Great Lakes 22, 25, 40, 72
Great Plains 24, 58

Harlem 35, 36
Hawaii 23, 86–8
Hiwassee Dam and River 75
Hoban, James 29
Hollywood 74
Holston River 74
Honolulu 87
Hoover Dam 47
Houston 66
Hudson River 25

ice floes 25
Inauguration Day 30
Independence, War of 18
Indians, American 13, 61, 63, 64, 65
Irish 11
Italians 13

Japanese 9
Jazz 53
Juneau 83, 84

Lake Superior 40
Lanai 88
L'Enfant, Pierre Charles 27
Lincoln, Abraham 14, 30, 49, 51
Lindbergh, Charles 80
Lone Star State 66
Los Angeles 10, 23, 74
Louisiana 51, 53
Louisiana Purchase 52, 53

Manhattan 34
Mardi Gras 53, 54
Mississippi River 37, 38
Missouri River 37, 38

Mormons 45
motels 43

Negroes 14, 36, 76, 78
New Amsterdam 34
New Orleans 9, 49, 51, 52, 53
New York 10, 11, 12, 23, 32, 33, 34, 35
Nob Hill 69
Nome 84, 85

Ohio 37, 74
oil 66, 85–6
"Old Glory" 20

Penn, William 16
Pentagon 29
pineapples 88
Poles 72, 73
Potomac River 27
Prohibition 71, 72

railways 41, 44
rainfall line 26, 27
"Redcoats" 29
Representatives, House of 31
Rio Grande 37, 39
Rocky Mountains 22, 37, 38, 39, 44, 46
"Russian Hill" 10

St Lawrence Seaway 40
Salt Lake City 46, 47
Sandwich Islands 86
San Francisco 10, 67, 68, 69
segregation 76, 78
sequoia trees 26
Sierra Nevada 24
Sioux Indians 62
Sitting Bull 63
slavery 49, 50, 51
spacecraft 66
space travel 79
Spaniards 44
sport 89–91
"Staked Plains" 24
Stars and Stripes 20
Stowe, Harriet Beecher 50
sugar 88

Tea Act 18
Tennessee River 75
Tennessee Valley 74, 75
Texas 66
Times Square 35
time zones 23

Uncle Tom's Cabin 50
Union flag 18, 20
United Nations 33

Vinland 16
Virginia 16

Washington, 27, 29, 30, 31
Washington, George 20, 27
Wayne, Mad Anthony 71
White House 29
Wild West 58, 60, 66
Winthrop, John 17
Wright Brothers 79, 80